11.45

A New True Book

VOTING AND ELECTIONS

By Dennis B. Fradin

CHILDRENS PRESS ™

CHICAGO

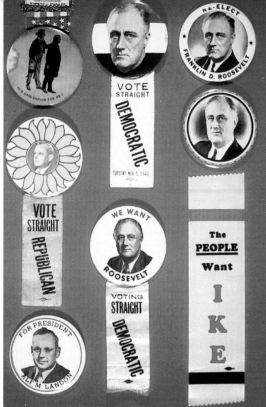

Collection of campaign buttons

PHOTO CREDITS

Roloc Color Slides—2, 4 (top), 10, 14 (bottom left and right), 16 (2 photos), 25 (top left and right), 30, 38 (left), 42

Wide World—Cover, 4 (bottom left and right), 17, 18 (2 photos), 19, 21, 25 (bottom), 26 (2 photos), 37 (right), 38 (right), 40

Cameramann International—6

Historical Pictures Service, Chicago—8 (2 photos), 13

Hillstrom Stock Photo:
© Art Brown—14 (top)
© Richard L. Capps—23, 29, 31 (left)
© American Film Productions—31 (right)
©Norma Morrison—33, 35, 45

Frost Publishing Group—15

Nawrocki Stock Photo:
© Ken Sexton—37 (left)

Cover—A political convention in the U.S.A.

Library of Congress Cataloging in Publication Data

Fradin, Dennis B.
  Voting and elections.

  (A New true book)
  Includes index.
  Summary: A brief history of elections and voting and an explanation of how these procedures work in the United States today.
  1. Elections—Juvenile literature. 2. Voting—Juvenile literature. [1. Elections. 2. Voting]
I. Title.
JF1001.F73 1985   324.9   85-7715
ISBN 0-516-01274-6   AACR2

TABLE OF CONTENTS

People who live in democratic countries, such as the United States (above) or India (below and right), vote for the people they want to lead their country.

WHAT IS VOTING?

Two people want to be the leader of a classroom, town, or country. "I'm best for the job!" says the first person. "No, *I'm* best!" says the second. How do the other people decide who their leader will be?

In many places they have elections. Each

A truck covered with election posters drives through a neighborhood.

person studies the names
on a ballot and then votes.
The ballots are counted.
The person with the most
votes for a job is the
winner.

THE FIRST VOTERS

The earliest people had to fight wild animals and other tribes to survive. In those early times, the best fighters became the leaders.

The Greeks were among the first known voters. About 2,500 years ago the Greeks began voting to choose some public officials and to decide some law cases. Usually

A Roman (left) casts his vote. The "A" marked on the ballot showed the voter approved, or voted "Yes." To keep people from voting twice the Romans made the voters cross a narrow bridge, one by one, to cast their votes.

they voted by raising their hands. Sometimes they selected black or white pebbles to show their choices.

The Romans, more than 2,000 years ago, also decided some issues by voting. However, the Greeks and Romans did not vote often, and they allowed only a few people to vote.

From the time of Christ all the way to the 1700s, most of the world was ruled by kings and queens. The word of a king or queen was law. People could not vote or even express their opinions to these rulers.

During the 1700s, people in many countries rebelled

The Boston Tea Party: Not allowed to vote, the American colonists showed King George III of England how much they hated the tax on tea by dumping it into Boston Harbor.

against their leaders. In 1775 the American people rebelled against England's King George III. In France the people rebelled against King Louis XVI in 1789. The people in both countries then faced a big problem. How would they make decisions? They decided that voting was the answer.

In the early 1790s people in France voted to elect their leaders. However, only the richer Frenchmen were allowed to vote. Those who didn't own property or pay taxes couldn't vote. The same was true in the United States.

HISTORY OF U.S. VOTING

Few people were
allowed to vote in the
early years of the United
States. Poor people, blacks,
women, and Indians
couldn't vote. The only
ones who *could* vote were
wealthy white men. This
situation lasted a
surprisingly long time.

Each group battled—with
words and sometimes even
with weapons—to gain the

Blacks voting in New Orleans, Louisiana

legal right to vote. In the 1800s, white males who were not wealthy won the right to vote. Black males won voting rights in 1870 with the passage of the Fifteenth Amendment to

Women across the country finally won the right to vote in 1920. They worked hard to get the vote with fund-raising and publicity activities (above). Cartoons and posters of the time (below) show that many people were uncomfortable with the idea of women voting.

Abigail Duniway registers to vote in Oregon in 1913 after fighting for women's voting rights in that state.

the Constitution. Women won voting rights in 1920, when the Nineteenth Amendment was passed. The Indians, the first people to live in what is now the United States, weren't allowed to vote in every state until 1948.

An artist's tribute to the passage of the Civil Rights Act, giving blacks the right to vote (above). A button showing President Theodore Roosevelt and black educator Booker T. Washington (right)

Even with the legal right to vote, some Americans were often stopped from voting. In the late 1800s and early 1900s, several states made it difficult for black people to vote. The U.S. government had to pass more laws to make

Blacks registering to vote in Charleston, South Carolina

sure that blacks could vote.

Until recently, Americans had to be at least twenty-one years old to vote in most states. Many people thought it was unfair that people who were eighteen

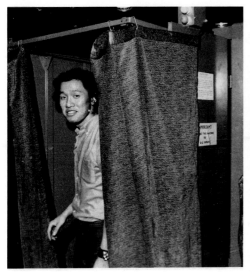

Two eighteen-year-olds
voting for the first time

to twenty years old had to
fight in wars but weren't
allowed to vote. In 1971
the Twenty-sixth
Amendment was passed. It
lowered the voting age to
eighteen.

Eight Democrats running for president in 1984

FREE ELECTIONS

A free and honest election is based on two conditions. People must have a choice of candidates, and they must be allowed to vote in secret.

In countries ruled by

dictators, often no one is allowed to vote. When elections are held in such countries, they usually are "fixed," or decided in advance. For example, the people may be given a ballot with just one name on it. If there is a choice of candidates, the voters may be told which one to choose. They may also have to show their marked ballots to government officials. People who don't

Citizens of El Salvador, shown here lined up to cast their ballots, are required by law to vote.

vote as they were ordered may be punished.

Today, many countries have free elections. But there are still some that have "fixed" elections or no elections at all.

THE VOTING PROCESS IN THE UNITED STATES

Each country has its own laws about voting. Here is the way voting in the United States works.

Before people can vote, they must register. Then their names are placed on the lists of people who may vote. People can register at such places as a city clerk's or county

Registering to vote in a school gym

clerk's office. In most
states people must register
just once—before voting
for the first time—unless
he or she moves.

Most voters want to learn about the men and women who are running for office. These persons, called candidates, give speeches and meet with voters before elections. In elections for major offices, candidates may debate on TV and radio. They may also have TV, radio, and newspaper ads. They have posters made and pass out buttons.

Candidates help people learn about what they
stand for through posters (above), campaign
buttons (left), and public debates (below).

Democratic President Andrew Jackson used the donkey as a symbol of his party after being called a "jackass" by his opponents. A nineteenth-century cartoonist first used the elephant to represent the Republican party.

In the United States, most candidates for public office belong to one of the two main political groups, or parties. These are the

Democratic party and the Republican party.

Usually, several Democrats and several Republicans want to win a particular office. Voters might be confused by a long list of candidates. To slim down the list, primary elections are held before the regular election day. The Democrat who receives the most votes from his or her party's voters in a primary election becomes the Democratic candidate on election day. The Republican who receives the most votes becomes the Republican candidate.

On election day there will be one Democratic and one Republican candidate for each office on the ballot. There also may be candidates who belong to smaller political parties. Or there may be candidates who don't belong to any party.

ELECTION DAY!

On election day, the place where people in a neighborhood vote is called a polling place. Schools, churches, and other big buildings are used as polling places.

In a polling place, voters first have their names checked by the voting officials.

As voters enter their polling place, they tell their names to the election officials. The officials make sure the voters are registered. They check off the voters' names. That

Voters may receive a paper ballot
from voting officials (left).
Then they go into private booths
to mark their choices (above).

way they make certain
that no one votes twice!

Each voter enters a
private voting booth. Some
polling places have voting
machines inside the
booths. In that case, the
voters just pull levers to

show their choices. Other places use computerized ballots. To vote with these, voters must punch a hole next to a candidate's name. In still other places, voters use a pencil to make an X next to the name of their favorite candidate.

What about voters who don't like any of the candidates on the ballot? These voters can write in

Voters in these voting booths use computerized punch cards.

the names of people they
prefer.

During presidential
elections, there are always
a few people who write in
such names as "Donald
Duck" and "Mickey Mouse."

They do this to show that they are not happy with any of the candidates on the ballot. Voters are free to vote for anyone they want, but very few waste their votes in this way.

Besides electing people for public offices, voters may be asked to vote on other matters. They may be asked to vote on how they would feel about a tax increase or some other

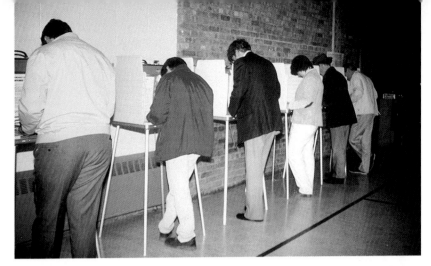

Citizens who want a voice in their government make a special effort to vote on election day.

issue. When voters are asked to give their opinions in this way, it is called a referendum. Voters may also be asked to decide whether or not certain judges should keep their jobs.

Once polling places close, the voting is over.

COUNTING THE VOTES

A correct vote count is very important. In fact, without it an election is useless.

When the polls close in the evening, the officials at each polling place count the votes. If paper ballots were used, they must count each one. With computerized ballots and voting machines, the totals are produced automatically.

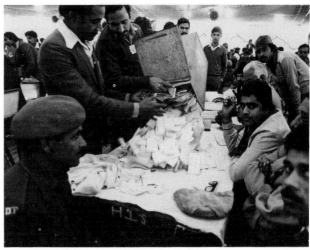

In the biggest general election in the world, ballots in New Delhi, India, were counted by hand (above). A computer counts computerized ballots (left).

The officials deliver the results to a central vote-counting place. This may be the office of a city clerk, a county clerk, or a board of elections. As the votes are counted, the results are given to TV,

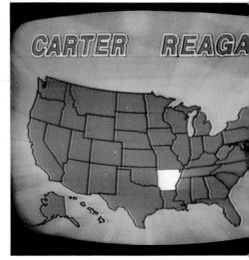

A national television studio (above) broadcasts election results all through the night after the polls close in a presidential election.

radio, and newspapers. Many people stay up all night to hear the election reports. Once all the votes have been counted, the winners are declared.

Elections for some offices are more complicated than this. For example, U.S. citizens vote for president but don't directly elect the president. A group called the electoral college does this.

The people's votes for president are counted in each state. Electoral college members are expected to vote for the candidate who received the most votes within their state. This means that, although the members of the electoral college select

Each party holds a national convention
to select its candidate for president.

the president, they have
been told how to vote by
the people. So the
candidate for president
who receives the biggest
share of the people's vote
is usually the winner
anyway.

What if a candidate loses a close election and thinks that the votes weren't counted correctly? In many cases, he or she can go to court to ask for a recount. All the ballots are stored at a central office. Officials may have to recount each vote to make certain that the proper person is named the winner.

The Capitol in Washington, D.C., decorated for the
inauguration of the newly-elected president

THE IMPORTANCE OF VOTING

More than two hundred years ago, Benjamin Franklin said that voting is "the common right of freemen." Women couldn't vote in Franklin's time. Today he would say voting is the right of all women, too!

Countries in which the people take part in government are called democracies. One of the best ways for people to express their views in a democracy is by voting. When people vote, they help decide who their leaders will be, how much taxes they should pay, and how the tax money will be spent.

When you reach the
legal age, you should vote.
Perhaps one day you
might even run for office!

WORDS YOU SHOULD KNOW

amendment(ah • MEND • ment) — a change in the law

ballot(BAL • ut) — the list of names and offices on which voters make their choices

candidates(KAN • dih • dayts) — people who are running for a certain office or position

computerized(kum • PYOO • ter • ized) — relating to computers

debate(dih • BAYT) — a discussion in which several people give opinions and argue over issues

democracy(dem • OCK • ruh • see) — a form of government in which the people take an active role in decision making

Democratic party(dem • oh • KRAT • ik PAR • tee) — one of the two main political parties in the United States

dictator(DIK • tay • ter) — a ruler whose word is law

election(ih • LEK • shun) — the process by which people choose their leaders by voting

electoral college(ih • LEK • tor • el KAHL • ij) — the group that elects the president of the United States based on the votes of the people

fixed election(FIXD ih • LEK • shun) — an election in which the outcome has been decided in advance

legal(LEE • gil) — relating to the law

political parties(puh • LIT • ik • il PAR • teez) — organizations, such as the Democrats and the Republicans, which work to get their candidates elected

polling place — the place where people in a neighborhood vote

primary election(PRY • mair • ee ih • LEK • shun) — an election held before election day to slim down the list of candidates

recount(REE • kownt) — counting the votes for a second time

referendum(ref • er • REN • dum) — the process in which voters express their opinions on an issue before a law is passed

registration(reh • jis • TRAY • shun) — the process by which a person's name is placed on an official list of voters

Republican party(rih • PUB • lih • kin PAR • tee) — one of the two main political parties in the United States

voting(VOH • ting) — a method by which people choose among several alternatives

write-in candidates(RITE • in KAN • dih • dayts) — candidates whose names have to be written in because they are not printed on the ballot

INDEX

About the Author

*Dennis Fradin attended Northwestern University on a partial
creative writing scholarship and was graduated in 1967. He has
published stories and articles in such places as* Ingenue, The
Saturday Evening Post, Scholastic, Chicago, Oui, *and* National
Humane Review. *His previous books include the Young People's
Stories of Our States series for Childrens Press, and* Bad Luck
Tony *for Prentice-Hall. In the True book series Dennis has written
about astronomy, farming, comets, archaeology, movies, space
colonies, the space lab, explorers, and pioneers. He is married and
the father of three children.*